A Pocketbook of Encouragement

Rachelle C. Bourassa

A POCKETBOOK OF ENCOURAGEMENT
Copyright © 2018 by Rachelle C. Bourassa

Unless otherwise noted, bible verses are taken from the New King James Version®. Copyright © 1982 by Thomas Nelson, Inc. Used by permission. All rights reserved. Scripture quotations marked NLT are taken from the Holy Bible, New Living Translation, copyright © 1996, 2004, 2007 by Tyndale House Foundation. Used by permission of Tyndale House Publishers, Inc., Carol Stream, Illinois 60188. All rights reserved. Scripture quotations marked TPT are from The Passion Translation®. Copyright © 2017, 2018 by Passion & Fire Ministries, Inc. Used by permission. All rights reserved. ThePassionTranslation.com. Scripture quotations designated (NET) are from the NET Bible® copyright ©1996–2018 by Biblical Studies Press, L.L.C. http://netbible.com All rights reserved. Scripture quotations marked MSG are taken from The Message. Copyright © by Eugene H. Peterson 1993, 1994, 1995, 1996, 2000, 2001, 2002. Used by permission of NavPress Publishing Group. Scripture quotations marked AMP are taken from the Amplified® Bible, Copyright © 1954, 1958, 1962, 1964, 1965, 1987 by The Lockman Foundation. Used by permission. Scripture taken marked NIrV are taken from the HOLY BIBLE, NEW INTERNATIONAL READER'S VERSION®. NIrV®. Copyright © 1994, 1996 by International Bible Society. Used by permission of Zondervan. All rights reserved.

Printed in Canada

ISBN: 978-1-4866-1742-5

Word Alive Press
119 De Baets Street, Winnipeg, MB R2J 3R9
www.wordalivepress.ca

Cataloguing in Publication may be obtained through Library and Archives Canada

To those who showed compassion to me and played a role in my journey of recovery

Introduction

I want to begin by saying that Jesus (Yeshua) is the inspiration for my writing. His life and death have given me strength and courage to do something I have never done before—write a book. My heart for you is that you would be able to receive an infilling of the compassion spoken of in the Bible and the anointing that breaks every yoke (Isaiah 10:27), and experience His healing.

I write from my personal experiences and give Yeshua all the glory in times of hardship, and in times of victory. There is hope in Him.

> *I would have lost heart, unless I had believed that I would see the goodness of the Lord in the land of the living.*
> —Psalm 27:13

I have tasted and seen His goodness, and I pray that you will, as well.

Day One

IN 2003, I EXPERIENCED A STRANGE TRAUMA THAT SENT ME ON A mental and emotional downward spiral. I was stung by a bee while camping and thought I was having an allergic reaction, but by the time I got to the hospital several hours later, I had allowed fear to take hold of me. It wasn't an allergic reaction, and by that point, my adrenaline levels wouldn't stabilize.

For days, weeks, and months, I couldn't sleep or focus. I suffered anxiety attacks, which I had never experienced before. I couldn't be in public; I couldn't even do simple tasks, like prepare a meal.

Looking back, years after the ordeal, I would call this post-traumatic stress disorder.

I had never felt so alone, isolated, out of control, fearful, hopeless, discouraged and in such despair. My mom had passed away at the age of fifty-three in 1995, and I was convinced that I, too, would die at an early age.

My friends and family rallied around me in prayer, even though I couldn't receive them. I made trips to my doctor every week for weeks on end. I'm thankful he was a Christian from our church, and he even prayed with me during several examinations. I was convinced there was nothing anybody could do but watch me slowly fade away.

That should have been my first clue. It was the biggest lie I've ever believed—that I was going to die.

> *Give ear to my prayer, O God, and do not hide Yourself from my supplication. Attend to me, and hear me; I am restless in my complaint, and moan noisily... My heart is severely pained within me, and the terrors of death have fallen upon me.*
>
> —Psalm 55:1–2, 4

Day Two

SOMETIMES EVENTS HAPPEN IN A FLASH, BUT SOMETIMES THEY transpire over a long period of time. Regardless of how things were for me, or how things are for you today, I believe you have picked up this book for a reason.

These are a few scriptures that echo where my heart was: hopeless and lost.

> *I am as good as dead, like a strong man with no strength left. They have left me among the dead, and I lie like a corpse in a grave. I am forgotten, cut off from your care.*
>
> —Psalm 88:4–5b, NLT

> *He has buried me in a dark place, like those long dead. He has walled me in, and I cannot escape. He has bound me in heavy chains.*
>
> —Lamentations 3:6–7, NLT

> *Terrors overwhelm him like a flood; at night a whirlwind carries him off.*
>
> —Job 27:20, NET

No, I didn't truly want to be carried off, even though the water was rising and I felt like I was going to drown. No, I didn't actually want to drown, but how would I avoid it

Picture a cliff, with someone hanging over the edge, hanging on with the last bit of strength he or she has. That's where I was, and I just wanted to let go; yet I knew I didn't want to drown. Could I, or would I, give up?

Is that where you are?

Rachelle C. Bourassa

Hear my cry, O God; Attend to my prayer. From the end of the earth I will cry to You, when my heart is overwhelmed; Lead me to the rock that is higher than I.

—Psalm 61:1–2

Father, I pray that my words will make a difference today.

Day Three

Psalms 120 to 134 are called the songs of ascent. They move upward, like a piano scale. In the same way, we were created to continue moving upward into God's presence, always moving up into His open, welcoming arms.

While I was in Israel, our tour bus was slowly making its way into Jerusalem. It was a long, subtle, winding climb upward. This climb into the city of Jerusalem is parallel to the rise of the human soul finding its way to God.

As we made our way into the city, our group began to sing those songs of ascent. Interestingly, they begin in a very dark place. *"In my distress I cried to the Lord, and He heard me. Deliver my soul, O Lord, from lying lips and from a deceitful tongue"* (Psalm 120: 1–2).

But as we climb, the verses becomes lighter and lighter.

I will lift up my eyes to the hills—From whence comes my help? My help comes from the Lord, who made heaven and earth. He will not allow your foot to be moved; He who keeps you will not slumber.
—Psalm 121:1–3

If it had not been the Lord who was on our side. . . then they would have swallowed us alive.
—Psalm 124:1, 3

Those who trust in the Lord are like Mount Zion, which cannot be moved, but abides forever.
—Psalm 125:1

Rachelle C. Bourassa

O Lord, who could stand? But there is forgiveness with You, that You may be feared. I wait for the Lord, my soul waits, and in His word I do hope.

—Psalm 130:3–5

Over the course of time, as Jesus came to me through people and His Word, I began to see that He didn't want me to stay in that dark place. He was reaching out to me.

Day Four

> *I call heaven and earth as witnesses today against you, that I have set before you life and death, blessing and cursing; therefore choose life, that you and your descendants may live.*
>
> —Deuteronomy 30:19

AT THIS POINT, I WAS STILL BELIEVING THE LIE (THAT I WAS GOING TO die), but I was seeing a ray of hope encouraging me to want something different. I had to choose to want it. I had to choose life. Choosing to keep going was difficult for me; it might also be difficult for you.

After several months of doctor visits, two things happened together that helped me. My doctor suggested taking an antidepressant for a short while, and someone gave me an audiotape on the spirit of fear. For the next month, I faithfully took my pill and listened to the tape repeatedly.

> *For God did not give us a spirit of timidity or cowardice or fear, but He has given us a spirit of power and of love and of sound judgment and personal discipline (abilities that result in a calm, well-balanced mind and self-control).*
>
> —2 Timothy 1:7, AMP

That was the scripture on which the teaching was based. My doctor encouraged me to say it out loud so that my head and ears could hear my voice declaring this truth (maybe hundreds of times a day) until my heart actually received it as truth.

Yes, I have *not* been given a spirit of fear. Yes, I have *not* been given a spirit of fear! I had to choose life. I had to choose to believe the scripture was true.

I'm asking you to make the same choice. I'm asking you to choose life today. My heart is urging you to desire something better than what is floating around you, to want to get out of this dark place.

Day Five

For weeks and months, I continued to say to myself, "You, Rachelle, have not been given a spirit of fear but of power, love, and a sound mind." I slowly began to believe it and these words began to open some light on the path ahead of me that I could trust and walk on.

I encourage you to begin vocalizing that scripture into your atmosphere. These words will bring some of the light that you need into the dark place in which you may find yourself.

We were not created to be alone. God wants our fellowship, and He wants us to be in fellowship with others. Look around you and focus on the people you have in your life. Even though you may not have any ability to even want to be with people at this time, do something that will help you recognize them. Write a list with one or two things about each one. Look at photos or even the telephone book. Remind yourself how important each one is to you.

I'm so thankful for my husband. He walked with me even when he had no idea how. Sometimes he let me do nothing, but sometimes he pushed me a little bit in the direction of keeping connected to people. That helped me.

> *A person standing alone can be attacked and defeated, but two can stand back-to-back and conquer. Three are even better, for a triple-braided cord is not easily broken.*
>
> —Ecclesiastes 4:12, NLT

> *Father of all mercy! God of all healing counsel! He comes alongside us when we go through hard times, and before you know it, he brings us*

alongside someone else who is going through hard times so that we can
be there for that person just as God was there for us.

—2 Corinthians 1:4, MSG

Day Six

For You will light my lamp; The Lord my God will enlighten my darkness.

—Psalm 18:28

For with You is the fountain of life; in Your light we see light.
—Psalm 36:9

Send me your light and your faithful care. Let them lead me. Let them bring me back to your holy mountain, to the place where you live.
—Psalm 43:3, NIrV

LIGHT IS VERY POWERFUL. ONE SINGLE LITTLE CANDLE CAN GET RID OF a lot of darkness. That small bit of light can make the difference between being paralyzed and unable to move, to being able to find your way out of the darkness slowly but surely.

It's prudent for me to stop here and introduce you—if you do not already know Him—to the true Light, Jesus the Messiah (Yeshua), the son of God, the Light of the world.

Jesus once again addressed them; 'I am the world's Light. No one who follows me stumbles around in the darkness. I provide plenty of light to live in.

—John 8:12, MSG

That was the true Light which gives light to every man coming into the world... But as many as received Him, to them He gave the right to become children of God, to those who believe in His name: who were born, not of blood, nor of the will of the flesh, nor of the will of man, but of God.

—John 1:9, 12–13

Choose life. Don't give up. Choose light, not darkness and despair.

Day Seven

The people who sat in darkness have seen a great light, and upon those who sat in the region and shadow of death Light has dawned.

—Matthew 4:16

JESUS HAS DAWNED. I PROCLAIM THAT OVER YOU RIGHT NOW: LIGHT HAS dawned over you. *The* Light, Yeshua, has dawned over you. His great light is opening a tiny path ahead of you today. Let's take that path together in the steps of this journal.

We (you and I) were in a very dark place, but now we've received some light that's been shed on our road ahead of us, and now we can begin the climb up that holy mountain where God lives.

I have experienced firsthand what it feels like to be in a very dark place and make a journey out of it into a marvelous light. I truly experienced a victory over the fear of death, and now I am no longer afraid to die; even more than that, I can recognize fear and now am equipped with victory to overcome it. I can truly declare, I will live and not die, and work out my days to declare the wonders of the Lord. *"I shall not die, but live, And declare the works of the Lord"* (Psalm 118:17). Amen.

I would have lost heart, unless I had believed that I would see the goodness of the Lord In the land of the living.

—Psalm 27:13

Father, I ask for a newness for the reader to understand the power of the choice of life, in Jesus' name.

Rachelle C. Bourassa

Day Eight

Bless the Lord, O my soul; And all that is within me, bless His holy name! Bless the Lord, O my soul, and forget not all His benefits: Who forgives all your iniquities, who heals all your diseases, who redeems your life from destruction, who crowns you with lovingkindness and tender mercies.

—Psalm 103:1–4

THERE'S A KEY TRUTH IN THIS PSALM, AND IN MANY OTHER SCRIPTURES as well. It's the life that's in our spoken word. The "you" in the psalm is me, my soul. The reality is that there is life for me when I speak to myself. The scripture is reminding me to remind myself of God's goodness, of His mercies, of His capabilities, of His faithfulness, of His desire to redeem my life from destruction. He really wants the best for me. He really wants the best for *you*. *"The Lord executes righteousness and justice for all who are oppressed"* (Psalm 103:6).

Wow! I was oppressed, and He executed justice for me. He wants to do that for you, too.

I'm asking you to begin to speak—even sing—this Psalm over yourself, at least several times a day, until your heart begins to believe it's true. He really wants to redeem your life from destruction.

Thank You, Lord.

Day Nine

God is our refuge and strength, A very present help in trouble, therefore we will not fear.

—Psalm 46:1–2a

THE CIRCUMSTANCES AROUND US MIGHT LOOK DAUNTING WITH OUR physical eyes, creating fear, but this scripture tells us that we can take refuge in God in the midst of our trouble; therefore, we don't have to believe or be afraid of what we see.

Have you heard of the acronym for fear, "False Evidence Appearing Real?" This is the kind of fear we need to say "no" to. We don't want to see things that might look good and find out later that they were false. We want the fear of the Lord. We want to discern with the mind of Christ because He knows all things.

For instance, the Bible tells us that we are fearfully and wonderfully made. We can certainly stumble trying to put that truth into our day-to-day lives; sometimes we make mistakes, sometimes we make terrible choices, sometimes we mess up, and yet God says we're wonderful! Wow.

"Through the Lord's mercies we are not consumed, Because His compassions fail not. They are new every morning; Great is Your faithfulness" (Lamentations 3:22–23). The Lord's compassions for us *never* fails. Never is a very long time! We need those compassions to see us the way He sees us. According to His Word, we are fearfully and wonderfully made. Don't look at yourself with your human eyes, but for now, look with the eyes of your heart, and simply receive this truth.

God says I am fearfully and wonderfully made. God loves and cares for me simply because I am His creation. He loves and cares for me simply because He is good.

Rachelle C. Bourassa

Day Ten

IN THE DAYS AHEAD, I WANT TO LAY A FOUNDATION OF GOD'S goodness, grace, and ever-present hand stretched out to us in *all* times, good and bad.

Oh give thanks to the Lord, for He is good! For His mercy endures forever.

—Psalm 106:1, 107:1

The truth is that God is good—He truly is a good father. We can call on Him; we can trust Him; we can be assured He will respond to us in our times of trouble. Read the following scriptures that describe God's goodness to us:

I love the Lord, because He has heard my voice and supplications. Because He has inclined His ear to me, therefore I will call upon Him as long as I live.

—Psalm 116:1–2

Blessed is he who comes in the name of the Lord! We have blessed you from the house of the Lord. God is the Lord, and He has given us light... You are my God, and I will praise You. You are my God, I will exalt You. Oh, give thanks to the Lord, for He is good! For His mercy endures forever.

—Psalm 118:26–29

Then they cried out to the Lord in their trouble, and He saved them out of their distresses. He brought them out of darkness and the shadow of death, and broke their chains in pieces.

—Psalm 107:13–14

Hear my prayer, O Lord, and let my cry come to You. Do not hide Your face from me in the day of my trouble; Incline Your ear to me; In the day that I call, answer me speedily.

—Psalm 102:1b–2

Father, I ask that You reveal Yourself to the reader through these scriptures today, that they may experience Your goodness, in Yeshua's name. Amen.

Rachelle C. Bourassa

Day Eleven

I love God's Word. In it we find so much life. Even when we don't know what to do or where to find help for our situation, we can look to the Holy Spirit for guidance at any time.

Reading, studying, and declaring God's Word, especially the books of Psalms and Proverbs, on a regular basis is a good practice for receiving God's guidance and faithfulness.

So far, I have given you two of the major words of life that I needed to come out of my place of darkness—2 Timothy 1:7 (fear) and Psalm 27:13 (losing heart). By now, on Day Eleven, I am prayerful that you have also received a word from the Lord that is shining light on your path. God is faithful, and He is good.

He sent His word and healed them, and delivered them from their destructions. Oh, that men would give thanks to the Lord for His goodness, and for His wonderful works to the children of men!
—Psalm 107:20–2

My story is one of healing. I want to see the Lord send out His Word and heal you, delivering you from your destructions.

I'm going to give you some "homework." Find an online resource, such as e-Sword, a free Bible study for PC computers, to help you go through the Bible looking for scriptures about healing—about our heavenly Father restoring health and wholeness to His people.

Lord, let the reader find something dynamic in their search today. Let their search bring another measure of deliverance, healing, and light to their path. We give You thanks in advance for Your goodness. Amen.

Day Twelve

Then I called on the name of the Lord: "Please, Lord, save me!" How kind the Lord is! How good he is! So merciful, this God of ours! The Lord protects those of childlike faith; I was facing death, and He saved me.

—Psalm 116:4–6, NLT

The name of the Lord is a strong tower; The righteous run to it and are safe.

—Proverbs 18:10

ALONG THIS JOURNEY, WE'VE BEEN SEEKING AND CALLING OUT TO GOD, first for help, then for understanding, and then for direction and a way out of our mess. I pray you've come to see that He truly is out there, that He hears your calling. He wants you to know that He is there and that He hears you.

The name of the Lord is a strong tower. Think of a significant manmade tower, like the Eiffel Tower in Paris. Now consider that the name of our Lord (Yeshua), Jesus, is much stronger than that, taller than that, higher than that, and a much greater source of protection than that!

The righteous run to it and are safe. We can run into the name of the Lord, Jesus, which provides a safety far beyond any fortified structure that's been known to man. This truth could easily go right over our heads because it's just too big. I have only ever seen a glimpse of this reality yet, but I pray that you, too, will get to see something that tells you that this is the truth.

Let my soul be at rest again, for the Lord has been good to me.

—Psalm 116:7, NLT

Rachelle C. Bourassa

Day Thirteen

But I called on your name, Lord, from deep within the pit. You heard me when I cried, "Listen to my pleading! Hear my cry for help!" Yes, you came when I called; you told me, "Do not fear."
—Lamentations 3:55–57, NLT

Our help is in the name of the Lord, who made heaven and earth.
—Psalm 124:8

How are you feeling today? We have been climbing together out of a dark place. Remember, we have not been given a spirit of fear. He tells us not to fear, but to be of good courage. Our help comes in the name of the Lord. I ask you again, how are you feeling? Have you felt the dark cloud lift yet? If not, continue to cry out for help in the name of the Lord. If so, continue to cry out in the name of the Lord! Either way, our help comes from Him.

But to you who fear my name the Sun of Righteousness shall arise with healing in His wings.

—Malachi 4:2a

Our journey together is one of rising out of darkness. As we sense the element of rising, we must also be mindful that He is also rising to do His part—the supernatural part. The Son, Jesus, is rising with healing for you. As we call upon His name, the healing and help will come.

Lord, today I ask that You give my friend, the reader, a revelation of the dark cloud lifting and light taking its place, in Jesus' name.

Day Fourteen

See, God has come to save me. I will trust in him and not be afraid.
The Lord God is my strength and my song; he has given me victory.
—Isaiah 12:2, NLT

It's a new day. Each new day, we reach from the Lord's heavenly bank account for mercies and grace that we need for the day ahead. Today is no different, except that today I pray you begin to see with a new light that the darkness around you isn't so dark after all.

With each glimmer of hope, we will begin to "practice" the things we've talked about: choosing life, choosing not to be afraid, choosing to call on the name of the Lord, choosing to believe that things will get better.

Today, let's talk about choosing to trust God. Go back to Day One and read out loud all the scriptures I've provided right through to today, Day Fourteen. Pause. When you're done, can you tell yourself if you see, hear, or feel trust? This is the application of all that we've faced so far. Can we trust Him to actually do what He says? Are these just empty words, or are they life-giving, transformation words? Is the God who created heaven and earth breathing life into you and your circumstance?

Decide to say "yes," even if it's a step of faith and you're still unsure. I'm standing with you saying "yes" right now!

Father, today I ask that You release whatever is needed in this dear reader's heart to see and believe that You can be trusted; that Your words are *not* empty, but rather *full* of life, in Jesus' name.

Rachelle C. Bourassa

Day Fifteen

I am teaching you today—yes, you—so you will trust in the Lord.
—Proverbs 22:19, NLT

Who among you fears the Lord and obeys his servant? If you are walking in darkness, without a ray of light, trust in the Lord and rely on your God.
—Isaiah 50:10, NLT

LET ME GO BACK TO MY OWN STORY FOR A MINUTE. I TRULY BELIEVED I was walking in darkness without a ray of light. For as much as that wasn't the whole truth, it's what I believed to be true at the time. I'm thankful now that I'd formed a relationship with Him beforehand, so even though everything appeared dark, there was light on my path, giving me what I needed to pause and put my full trust in Him.

Some might say God is "way out there" and choosing all this God stuff is also "way out there." But that's really one definition of having faith. Now, trusting in Him is the journey we take that walks out that faith. By admitting He is there, He is right, He is good, He is faithful, and He cares, we declare our trust in this God whom we don't see with the naked eye. He is our refuge, which I define as "anyone who runs to God, will make it." Hallelujah!

You love him even though you have never seen him. Though you do not see him now, you trust him; and you rejoice with a glorious, inexpressible joy.
—I Peter 1:8, NLT

Day Sixteen

I rejoice at Your word as one who finds great treasure.
—Psalm 119:162

I'M BEGINNING TO GET EXCITED. I'M WALKING WITH YOU DURING THESE thirty days, a journey I experienced in 2004, when I started to see light and hope around me. *"The entrance of Your words gives light; It gives understanding to the simple"* (Psalm 119:130). It's building up to something. We're on a treasure hunt; the treasure is Him and His attributes, character, Word, goodness, and faithfulness. We were in a very dark place and now we've come into a new place of light. That's worth getting excited about!

But how are you doing? Have you been able to track God's goodness? Are you ready to choose to receive these truths and say, "I'm all in"?

> *He has torn the veil and lifted from me the sad heaviness of mourning.*
> *He wrapped me in the glory garments of gladness.*
> —Psalm 30:11b, TPT

> *You will show me the way of life, granting me the joy of your presence*
> *and the pleasures of living with you forever.*
> —Psalm 16:11, NLT

Thank You, Abba Father, for the continual pouring out of Your grace and goodness. Thank You for the light that shines on us. Thank You that we can believe You are trustworthy. We believe Your Word is true, and we believe we can put our trust in You. *"I would have lost heart, unless I had believed that I would see the goodness of the Lord in the land of the living"* (Psalm 27:13). Amen.

Rachelle C. Bourassa

Day Seventeen

Those who live in the shelter of the Most High will find rest in the shadow of the Almighty. This I declare about the Lord; He alone is my refuge, my place of safety; he is my God, and I trust him.
—Psalm 91:1–2, NLT

THE IMAGERY HERE IS VERY CLEAR AND DYNAMIC. THERE'S A HIDING place, a shield, shelter, a place of safety and refuge. Each place provides a measure of protection and security. A hiding place, or shelter, is like a den where you can run and hide. A shield covers the front of you. Refuge is what you seek if you are being chased or threatened.

Every one of those places can be found in God and in His Word. The outcome is safety and rest. It's quite interesting, but in our journey of being in a dark place, I believe we didn't fathom that it may have been a hiding place our Father was holding for us for safety or refining.

When I get a glimpse of a dark place, now that I have been delivered from this one, I'm quick to turn to Him. In my heart, I know He will help me—maybe not immediately or the way I think He should, but He *will* help me, and in the meantime, I am safe. Therefore, I put all my hope in Him.

You are my hiding place and my shield; I hope in Your word. . . Uphold me according to Your word, that I may live; And do not let me be ashamed of my hope.
—Psalm 119:114–116

Day Eighteen

This is the day the Lord has made; We will rejoice and be glad in it.
—Psalm 118:24

EVEN AS I WRITE THIS, I SENSE A HEAVY WING OF SAFETY. I'M INCLINED to lift it up and sneak under it for the warmth of heaven, the warmth of my Father and His love for me.

I admit that sometimes I want to stay here in this warmth and not face the cold, harsh world, but then God tells me to bring His warmth to others. So then, from this hiding place, I take His Word that's been planted in my heart and off I go. This book is my gift to you from my heavenly Father. He wanted you to be touched by His love, goodness, and compassion.

We can rejoice and be glad every day, because God cares so much for us that He sends whatever He knows we need to light our way. Today, let's bask in something warm. Take a hot bath. Have a hot cup of tea. Stand in a window where the sun is shining. Let the warmth of heaven wash over you like a warm blanket. Let the peace of the Almighty touch you in a new way.

> *Pour out all your worries and stress upon him and leave them there, for he always tenderly cares for you.*
> —I Peter 5:7, TPT

> *Now, may the Lord himself, the Lord of peace, pour into you his peace in every circumstance and in every possible way. The Lord's tangible presence be with you all.*
> —2 Thessalonians 3:16, TPT

Rachelle C. Bourassa

Day Nineteen

Give thanks to the Lord, for he is good! His faithful love endures forever.
—I Chronicles 16:34, NLT

And in the midst of everything be always giving thanks, for this is God's perfect plan for you in Christ Jesus.
—I Thessalonians 5:18, TPT

Let the message about Christ, in all its richness, fill your lives. Teach and counsel each other with all the wisdom he gives. Sing psalms and hymns and spiritual songs to God with thankful hearts.
—Colossians 3:16, NLT

WITH MY WHOLE HEART, I AM THANKFUL THAT GOD HAS WORKED IN my life. Being thankful is key to receiving healing. When we can express appreciation to God in the midst of trouble, it's like saying that He has it covered, even before we see the answer. It declares He's bigger than the problem and that the problem must submit to His authority or "bigness."

We're on our journey where we want to get intentional about thanking Him for taking us out of the dark place, thanking Him for the journey thus far, and thanking Him for the continued journey into healing and freedom—even if we don't see it or feel it.

Let's practice. Pray this prayer out loud: "Thank You, Father, Abba, Lord—thank You for bringing me this far. Thank You for shedding light on my dark path. Thank You for not forgetting about me. Thank You for Your love and faithfulness. Thank You for You. Thank You for yesterday, today, and tomorrow. Thank You."

Day Twenty

Thank you! Everything in me says "Thank you!" Angels listen as I sing my thanks. I kneel in worship facing your holy temple and say it again: "Thank you!" Thank you for your love, thank you for your faithfulness; most holy is your name, and most holy is your Word.
—Psalm 138:1–2, MSG

THIS SCRIPTURE PASSAGE, TAKEN FROM THE MESSAGE TRANSLATION, TIES in wonderfully with the practice of thankfulness we practiced yesterday. Verse three goes on to say, *"The moment I called out, you stepped in; you made my life large with strength"* (Psalm 138:3, MSG).

Being thankful causes God to show up, step in, and help us do our part. The NET (New English Translation) for verse three says, *"When I cried out for help, you answered me. You made me bold and energized me"* (Psalm 138:3, NET).

There is such a sense of victory in that statement. We were in a very dark place, but as we move toward Him and His ways, the excitement builds in that we are healing and we will walk, talk, live, think, and laugh again and see without the fog. That makes me thankful.

I'm asking you to believe me, but even if you don't, continue to practice being thankful. Write out lists of things for which you're thankful, then walk around your home, expressing that thankfulness out loud.

Lord, I thank You for my friend who has stayed with me these last twenty days, and I thank You that they are experiencing Your goodness and compassion. Amen.

Rachelle C. Bourassa

Day Twenty-One

Keep on giving your thanks to God, for he is so good! His constant, tender love lasts forever!

—Psalm 118:1, TPT

The Lord is my strength and my song; he has given me victory. Songs of joy and victory are sung in the camp of the godly. The strong right arm of the Lord has done glorious things!

—Psalm 118:14–15, NLT

Sing out your thanks to the Lord.

—Psalm 147:7a, NLT

I'M INTENTIONALLY USING A LOT OF SCRIPTURE IN THIS POCKETBOOK because life and light is in the Word of God. That's why it's so important for you to choose to "do" what I am writing and to "be" the Word.

As you read and reread the Word, and declare it out loud, it goes forth and accomplishes creative miracles around you. Most scripture is action-oriented and demands displaying action or "being." We're called to be active participants, not bystanders of the Word; we read it, we say it, we pray it, we digest it, we believe it, and we choose to live it.

Remember my encounter with the "fear" scripture (2 Timothy 1:7)? *"For God has not given us a spirit of fear, but of power and of love and of a sound mind."* I read those words repeatedly, but it was still my responsibility to declare them, and then let God do the rest. It was my demonstration of action that declared that I, Rachelle, have not been given a spirit of fear.

Lord, release my friend's voice to thank and praise You.

Day Twenty-Two

It is good to give thanks to the Lord, and to sing praises to Your name, O Most High; To declare Your lovingkindness in the morning, and Your faithfulness every night.

—Psalm 92:1–2

Let us come before His presence with thanksgiving; Let us shout joyfully to Him with psalms.

—Psalm 95:2

I WISH I COULD MEET YOU, GET TO KNOW YOU A LITTLE, ASK IF YOU have any questions, and pray with you, but that is not the purpose of this pocketbook. I'm writing this to stir you up into fully engaging in the Word of God. You and I can come together today across the miles and "come before His presence with thanksgiving" as I believe we've been doing all along our journey. Be reminded again today that you're not alone; we're on the same road and we're thankful.

I thank God for you. I thank God that you've listened to me so far. I thank Him that you're feeling some hope in the midst of your darkness. I thank Him that we can come into His presence like two young siblings making their way across a crowded room to lay hold of their father's hand.

I wrote this little pocketbook of encouragement to make a way for you to encounter God's heavenly compassion. *"And when Jesus went out He saw a great multitude; and He was moved with compassion for them, and healed their sick"* (Matthew 14:14).

Father, thank You for the healing You have done in this reader's life. May it be for Your glory.

Rachelle C. Bourassa

You answer our prayers with amazing wonders and with awe-inspiring displays of power. You are the righteous God who helps us like a father. Everyone everywhere looks to you, for you are the confidence of all the earth, even to the farthest islands of the sea.

—Psalm 65:5, TPT

Day Twenty-Three

I will praise the Lord at all times; my mouth will continually praise him.
—Psalm 34:1, NET

Enter his gates with thanksgiving, and his courts with praise! Give him thanks! Praise his name!
—Psalm 100:4, NET

Every day I will praise you! I will praise your name continually!
—Psalm 145:2, NET

PRAISE IS IMPORTANT. IT'S ONE OF GOD'S PRINCIPLES WITH WHICH WE often struggle. In our human thought, praise seems to be something we should do after something good happens—a cause-and-effect scenario. In fact, praise is something we should do even *before* we see an outcome.

Praise is our voice saying and declaring that we believe that God will act on our behalf, that He is more than capable of coming out stronger than the destruction we see around us, and that He is neither surprised nor necessarily concerned about the bad, but desires to see restoration and order.

I praise God for the work that He's doing in you. Do you see all that He's doing? Do you feel that He's done something to heal you? Perhaps not yet, but that's exactly when we should start to praise Him! That's exactly when the praise principle kicks in.

Praise You, Jesus, for this journey, praise You for Your faithfulness, praise You for going ahead of us and preparing a path of healing. Praise You, Jesus, for my friend; praise You for Your compassion that heals everything. Praise You for loving us so much!

Rachelle C. Bourassa

Let my mouth be filled with Your praise and with Your glory all the day.
—Psalm 71:8

Day Twenty-Four

PSALM 150 IS THE LAST OF THE BOOK OF PSALMS, AND IN IT are thirteen different mentions of praise in only six short verses. The Book of Psalms ends very powerfully with an appeal to praise the Lord.

In a general overview of the Book of Psalms, many times the writers would often cry out for help like—"Oh, woe is me," "My life is in shambles," "Where are you, God?", etc., and then by the end of the lament, they would realize that turning to God was their only hope, and praising Him actually proved to be their strength.

Psalm 150:6 pretty much says it all—*"Let everything that has breath praise the Lord"*—a simple and direct truth and principle that ends the journey of lament for the psalmists, and for us, too. Praise the Lord for His ways. Praise the Lord for His goodness.

> *And in that day you will say: Praise the Lord, call upon His name; Declare His deeds among the peoples, make mention that His name is exalted. Sing to the Lord, for He has done excellent things; This is known in all the earth.*
>
> —Isaiah 12:4–5

Abba Father, we praise You together today. You alone are holy, and You alone are worthy of our praise.

Rachelle C. Bourassa

Day Twenty-Five

Be anxious for nothing, but in everything by prayer and supplication, with thanksgiving, let your requests be made known to God.
—Philippians 4:6

AS WE BEGIN TO END OUR JOURNEY TOGETHER, LET'S TAKE A LOOK AT "resting" in Him. Being anxious for nothing is the charge given in the scripture above. But how do we do that in a world full of anxiety, trials, hardships, hate, evil, even the possibility of catastrophe? Had I mentioned this at the beginning of our journey, you might have given up on this book, assuming I didn't have a clue about life.

Being anxious for nothing is a practiced lifestyle. It's learning that God is real, digging in His Word, discovering His character, and believing that He can be trusted. I'm believing that this is exactly what you've done on this journey. I'm believing that you've come to realize that this is the truth.

Out of this practiced lifestyle, of being anxious for nothing, your confidence in God should be growing to a place where you can ask Him anything and know that He'll take care of it. Once you believe He'll do just that, you can move forward, not being anxious for those things anymore. You'll continue on your journey of being anxious for nothing, a journey of "resting" in His ability and not your own.

Lord, may my friend experience rest in You today, for Your glory. Amen.

Day Twenty-Six

Rejoice in the Lord always. Again I will say, rejoice!
—Philippians 4:4

MY HEART IS SUDDENLY FULL AS I SAY, "REJOICE!" YES, I REJOICE IN the Lord, but I also rejoice in *you*. You are loved. You are unique. You are special. You are valued. You are important. You are God's creation and you are delivered, healed, and restored! That's certainly worth rejoicing over.

However, you might not feel like rejoicing at all. You might not even be in a place to receive or believe some—or any—of what I've said. Let me tell you that hope is a very powerful act. It can propel and move us in ways we don't even understand. *"This hope is a strong and trustworthy anchor for our souls. It leads us through the curtain into God's inner place"* (Hebrews 6:19, NLT). *"And this hope will not lead to disappointment. For we know how dearly God loves us, because he has given us the Holy Spirit to fill our hearts with his love"* (Romans 5:5, NLT).

God heals your pain and comforts you in times of sorrow. *"He heals the brokenhearted and binds up their wounds"* (Psalm 147:3). I truly hope that He is healing you right now. I have faith that He is. *"Faith is the confidence that what we hope for will actually happen; it gives us assurance about things we cannot see"* (Hebrews 11:1, NLT).

Father, by the time we finish up our thirty days together, I ask You to look upon this dear reader and be moved with compassion and heal them, whether they see it today, or only in weeks or months ahead, in Jesus' name.

Rachelle C. Bourassa

Day Twenty-Seven

Therefore, my beloved and longed-for brethren, my joy and crown, so stand fast in the Lord, beloved... And the peace of God, which surpasses all understanding, will guard your hearts and minds through Christ Jesus.

—Philippians 4:1, 7

YOU ARE GOD'S CROWN AND JOY, HIS BELOVED. REACH UP AND TAKE hold of that truth. His desire for you is to be free, to be at peace with your journey from a dark place into His marvelous light. That peace is supposed to surpass our understanding. It's what you need it to be, but you can't understand it with your mind. You must choose to believe it's true and it's there for you.

I chose to believe it was there for me. There have been times when I've thought, "This can't be real. How can I be at peace in the chaos of this situation?" Only with God's peace is this possible.

Now may the Lord of peace himself give you his peace at all times and in every situation. The Lord be with you all.
—2 Thessalonians 3:16, NLT

May the Lord bless you and protect you. May the Lord smile on you and be gracious to you. May the Lord show you his favor and give you his peace.

—Numbers 6:24–26, NLT

I continue to rally with you as we come to the end of our time together. Let us praise His name together as the scripture encourages us to do. Praise You, Jesus!

Day Twenty-Eight

Praise the Lord! For it is good to sing praises to our (gracious and majestic) God; Praise is becoming and appropriate. . . Great is our (majestic and mighty) Lord and abundant in strength; His understanding is inexhaustible (infinite, boundless).

—Psalm 147:1, 5, AMP

Sing to Him, sing psalms to Him; Talk of all His wondrous works! Glory in His holy name; Let the hearts of those who rejoice who seek the Lord! Seek the Lord and His strength; Seek His face evermore!

—I Chronicles 16:9–11

I will sing to the Lord as long as I live; I will sing praise to my God while I have my being. May my meditation be sweet to Him; I will be glad in the Lord.

—Psalm 104:33–34

I will praise You, O Lord, among the peoples, and I will sing praises to You among the nations. For Your mercy is great above the heavens, and Your truth reaches to the clouds.

—Psalm 108:3–4

PSALM 71:14 TALKS ABOUT CONTINUED HOPE IN THE LORD AND praising Him every day. *"But I will hope continually, and will praise you yet more and more;" "While I stretch out, reaching for You, and daily add praise to praise"* (MSG).

Let your praise be vibrant and creative. Every day, there is something new for you in and from Him, and I pray that you're quick to give something new back to Him in your praise. I'm adding

Rachelle C. Bourassa

my voice to your song of praise; let's sing together and join the heavenly choir of unity that sing praises to Him.

Day Twenty-Nine

Lord, I will worship you with extended hands as my whole heart explodes with praise!

—Psalm 9:1a, TPT

What harm could a man bring to me? With God on my side I will not be afraid of what comes. The roaring praises of God fill my heart, and I will always triumph as I trust his promises.

—Psalm 56:4, TPT

How could I be silent when it's time to praise you? Now my heart sings out loud, bursting with joy—a bliss inside that keeps me singing, "I can never thank you enough!"

—Psalm 30:12, TPT

So I'm thanking you with all my heart, with gratitude for all you've done.

—Psalm 56:12a, TPT

Lord God, unlock my heart, unlock my lips, and I will overcome with my joyous praise!

—Psalm 51:15, TPT

TODAY, I'M PRAISING THE LORD. I PRAISE HIM FOR BRINGING US THIS far. I praise Him for bringing you into my writing. I praise Him for His compassion that moves Him to healing you. I praise Him for the grace and wisdom I needed to write this book. I praise Him for His goodness, His faithfulness, and His Word. I praise Him for meeting you in a very special way in the last month. I praise Him for

Rachelle C. Bourassa

sustaining you with the newly shed light on the road ahead of you. I praise Him. Let everything that has breath praise Him.

Healing and freedom are yours, in Jesus' name!

Day Thirty

The Lord bless you, and keep you (protect you, sustain you and guard you); The Lord make His face shine upon you (with favor), and be gracious to you (surrounding you with lovingkindness); The Lord lift up His countenance (face) upon you (with divine approval), and give you peace (a tranquil heart and life).

—Numbers 6:24–26, AMP

THIS IS CALLED THE AARONIC BLESSING, OR AARON'S BENEDICTION. The priests—the line of Aaron—were instructed by God to say these words over the people and then He, Himself, would bless them.

I have been honoured that you decided to take this journey with me. I will forever carry you in my heart, and I chose to leave you with the blessing of the priests and all my love.

I will go in the strength of the Lord God; I will make mention of Your righteousness, of Yours only.

—Psalm 71:16

Go, my friend, in the strength of the Lord! I celebrate you. I celebrate your willingness to walk with me through these scriptures. I celebrate with you in your restored hope. And I celebrate the newness of life that will follow you all your days.

Rachelle C. Bourassa